I helped save the earth

55 fun ways
kids can make
a world of difference

by
Michael O'Brian

BERKLEY BOOKS, NEW YORK

I HELPED SAVE THE EARTH

A Berkley Book / published by arrangement with
Boldface Publishing, Inc.

PRINTING HISTORY
Berkley trade paperback edition / April 1991

ISBN: 0-425-12830-X

Introduction

It seems like every day you hear something on radio or TV about air pollution, acid rain or global warming. There are also often stories about subjects like these in newspapers and magazines. On Earth Day thousands of people marched in big parades and carried signs, chanting about saving the earth, and they were all on TV. What are these things, anyway? And if the adults can't seem to do anything about it all, what can a kid do?

Many of the problems come down to one simple thing: pollution. People are polluting the planet they live on. They are polluting the air and the land and the water.

A little pollution doesn't seem like such a bad thing. You see the smoke coming out of the tail pipe on your family's car, and it goes up into the air and disappears. You finish painting a model airplane and pour the brush cleaner down the drain and it's gone. So what's the big deal?

The big deal is that all that stuff builds up. Global warming means that the gases from all the tail pipes of all the cars in the world stay in the air high above the earth. Just like the glass on a greenhouse, these gases let the sun's light and heat in, but keep the earth's heat from going back out into space. This makes the earth's temperature rise, causing drought and crop failure and making the oceans rise.

We throw away so much garbage that we are now running out of places to put it. And acid rain caused by smoke from cars and power plants is harmful to plants and wildlife. Water pollution from toxic waste kills animals and causes disease in humans.

But if all the adults and all the governments in the world can't solve these problems, what can kids do about it? How can just one kid help save the earth?

The answer is that *everybody* can help save the earth. Every single person in the world can make a difference.

The motto of the people who are already working to save the earth is: "Think globally, act locally." That means that you should worry about the earth, but you're not expected to save the whole thing by yourself. All you have to do is clean up your part of it. If everyone helps save his own little corner of the earth, then the earth will be a much better place to live now—and forever.

What can you do? You need to think about the things that you and your family do that pollute the air and the water and the earth. Then you need to find a way to cut it out. No one expects anyone to live without causing some pollution. We just need to stop causing so much that plants and animals and humans are harmed by it. The important thing is to get a lot closer to a cleaner and healthier planet.

You can help save the earth by doing a lot of little things around the house. On the following pages are 55 ways you can help save the earth. And on each page is a place for you to put a sticker as a reward to yourself for helping. You probably won't be able to do each and every thing. Depending on where you live, some of them won't be possible, or won't be a problem in your house. Just do the best you can. Don't forget to tell your parents and your brothers and sisters what you are doing, and why it is important. And get them to help you, too.

It doesn't even have to cost money to help save the earth. The things that you will read about in this book won't cost anything. Some will save money for you and your family. Recycling can even earn you money.

But your biggest reward for doing the things talked about in this book will be that *you* will have helped SAVE THE EARTH!

I helped save the earth

1. Find the Leaky Faucets in Your House

FACT:

A leaky faucet can waste 3,000 gallons of water a year.

WHAT TO DO:

Check all the faucets in your house. Check the ones outside, too, where the garden hose is. Make sure that it is turned off, then watch for a minute to make sure that there are no drips. If there are, get someone to fix it.

AWARD BADGE:

I check all the faucets in my house.

I Helped Save the Earth!

2. Find the Leaky Toilets in Your House

FACT:

A leaky toilet can waste 20,000 gallons of water a year. That's enough to fill up a swimming pool.

WHAT TO DO:

Ask an adult to give you some food coloring, and to lift the top off the toilet tank. Put in 10 or 15 drops of the food coloring, enough to color the water. Don't let anyone use that toilet for about 15 minutes. Then look in the toilet bowl to see if any of the colored water from the tank has leaked into the bowl. If it has, ask an adult to fix it.

AWARD BADGE:

I check all the toilets in my house for leaks.

I Helped Save the Earth!

3. Recycle Aluminum Cans

FACT:

It takes as much energy to make one new can as it does to make 20 recycled ones.

WHAT TO DO:

Start saving empty aluminum cans. Use a box or trash bag or a garbage can just for cans. Put it out of the way in a closet, the basement or in the garage. Ask everyone to help, and check the wastebaskets often to make sure no one forgot and threw out a can. You can donate the cans to a recycling drive, or turn them in for cash at your local recycling center.

AWARD BADGE:

I recycle aluminum cans.

I Helped Save the Earth!

4. Cut the Rings on Six-pack Holders

FACT:

The plastic six-pack soda-holder can blow into the water from picnic trash or from a landfill. They are invisible under water, and fish, sea animals or birds can get trapped in one of the rings and die.

WHAT TO DO:

Cut each ring of the plastic six-pack holder before you throw it away.

AWARD BADGE:

I cut the rings on six-pack holders before I throw them away.

I Helped Save the Earth!

5. Recycle Newspapers

FACT:

It takes 500,000 trees just to make the newspapers we read every Sunday.

WHAT TO DO:

Find a good place out of the way in the basement, a closet or the garage. Save your family's newspapers. Tie them up with twine or put them in brown paper grocery bags. Find out how to recycle newspapers in your area. In some places, you have to take them to a recycling center. (You might even get money for them. Ask!) In other places, you put them out on the curb on a certain day and they are picked up.

AWARD BADGE:

I recycle old newspapers.

I Helped Save the Earth!

6. Use Paper, Not Plastic

FACT:

It takes a whole tree to make about 500 brown paper grocery bags. But plastic bags are worse because they can't be recycled, and the plastic will never decompose.

WHAT TO DO:

Tell your parents to ask for paper, not plastic, when checking out at the supermarket. Then save the paper bags and take them back on your next shopping trip. A lot of stores will give you money back for each brown paper bag you bring back and use again. Or use a cloth shopping bag for small purchases.

AWARD BADGE:

We use paper, not plastic. And I save the bags and use them again.

I Helped Save the Earth!

7. Take a Shower, Not a Bath

FACT:

A bath uses about twice as much water as a shower.

WHAT TO DO:

Take a shower instead of a bath. And ask your parents about special low-flow shower heads that use less water.

AWARD BADGE:

I take showers instead of baths, and I make them as short as I can.

I Helped Save the Earth!

8. Find the Leaky Windows in Your House

FACT:

As much energy leaks out the windows in American homes as flows through the Alaskan pipeline in one year.

WHAT TO DO:

Feel around windows and doors for cold air coming in. With an adult, move a lighted candle around each window. If the candleflame flickers, cold air is coming in. Get someone to weatherstrip the leaks that you find.

AWARD BADGE:

I check all the windows in the house for air leaks.

I Helped Save the Earth!

9. Avoid Using Paper Towels

FACT:

Paper towels are made out of trees. The more paper towels you use, the more trees get cut down.

WHAT TO DO:

Use a sponge to clean up spills. Use a cloth towel to dry your hands. Save old and torn clothes to use as cleaning rags.

AWARD BADGE:

I don't use paper towels.

I Helped Save the Earth!

10. Turn Off the Water

FACT:

Americans use about 150 gallons of water per person every day.

WHAT TO DO:

Don't let the water run while you brush your teeth or wash dishes. Turn the faucet on just long enough to rinse off your toothbrush or the dishes, and turn it back off again. And don't let it run until it gets cold when you want a drink. Keep a bottle of water in the refrigerator.

AWARD BADGE:

I don't let the water run longer than necessary.

I Helped Save the Earth!

11. Use Less Water to Flush the Toilet

FACT:

It takes about 6 gallons of water to flush the toilet.

WHAT TO DO:

Fill an old plastic bottle with water. You may have to put some stones in it to weigh it down. Have an adult take the top off the toilet tank and help you put the bottle in the tank where it won't get in the way of the moving parts. With the jug in place, the water within stays there permanently and doesn't need to be replaced with new water. You will save up to a gallon of water with every flush.

AWARD BADGE:

I helped fix the toilet so that it uses less water.

I Helped Save the Earth!

12. Turn Out the Lights and Appliances When You Are Not Using Them

FACT:

The electric company burns coal to produce the energy that keeps your lights on. That burning coal gives off gases that cause the greenhouse effect and acid rain.

WHAT TO DO:

Turn off the lights when you leave the room. And turn off lights in the room that you really don't need. In the daytime, sit closer to the window to read instead of turning on a light. Turn off the TV or the stereo when you aren't watching or listening.

AWARD BADGE:

I turn off lights and appliances that I'm not using.

I Helped Save the Earth!

13. Dress for the Weather

FACT:

Most of the energy in our homes is used for heating and cooling. And we use a lot more than we have to.

WHAT TO DO:

Wear clothes that are right for the weather. In winter, wear a sweater or a sweatshirt instead of turning up the heat or complaining about being cold. Get everyone else to dress right, and your house will be more comfortable at a lower temperature. Wear lighter, cooler clothes in the summer and you won't have to use the air conditioning.

AWARD BADGE:

I dress right for the weather.

I Helped Save the Earth!

14. Water the Lawn Early in the Morning

FACT:

If you water the lawn in the middle of the day when the sun is hot, most of the water evaporates before it gets to the roots.

WHAT TO DO:

It is best to water the lawn in the coolest part of the day. Watering at night can cause lawn disease. The best time to water is early in the morning, before the sun gets hot.

AWARD BADGE:

I water the lawn early in the morning.

I Helped Save the Earth!

15. Give the Lawn a Lot of Water Every Third Day

FACT:

If you water the lawn a little bit every day, most of the water dries up before it gets to the roots.

WHAT TO DO:

Most newspapers have a watering schedule during the summer. You pick a symbol for your house, or go by the last two numbers in your address. Follow the newspaper directions for when to water, and how much. You can figure out how much water your lawn is getting by putting two or three empty tin cans on the lawn around the sprinkler and measuring how much water is in them after watering.

AWARD BADGE:

I follow the newspaper watering schedule.

I Helped Save the Earth!

16. Be Careful Watering the Lawn

FACT:

Americans use 500 billion gallons of water every week to water their lawns.

WHAT TO DO:

Don't waste water. Make sure the sprinkler isn't dumping a lot of water on the sidewalk or street or driveway. Don't water on windy days when the water gets blown away instead of falling on the lawn.

AWARD BADGE:

I make sure we don't waste when watering the lawn.

I Helped Save the Earth!

17. Open the Blinds and Curtains During the Day in the Winter

FACT:

Sun coming through the windows heats up the room. This is called passive solar heat.

WHAT TO DO:

Your house will be warmer in the wintertime if you open all the blinds and curtains to let in the sunlight, which warms the air in the room. Make sure you close them again at night. The extra layer of material over the windows acts as an insulation—helping to keep out the cold, and keep in the heat.

AWARD BADGE:

I check the blinds every day during the winter to make sure they are open.

I Helped Save the Earth!

18. Close the Blinds During the Day in the Summer

FACT:

The same solar heating that is good in the winter will make your air conditioner work harder in the summer.

WHAT TO DO:

Make sure that all the blinds or shades are closed on the side of the house where the sun is shining.

AWARD BADGE:

I make sure the blinds are closed on the sunny side of the house in the summer.

I Helped Save the Earth!

19. Clean or Change the Furnace Filter Every Month

FACT:

A dirty filter makes the furnace or air conditioner use more energy. This means more air pollution and global warming.

WHAT TO DO:

Ask an adult to help you clean or change the filter, and make sure that you remember to do it every month.

AWARD BADGE:

I remember to change the furnace filter every month.

I Helped Save the Earth!

20. Make Sure the Lamps in Your House Have the Best Bulbs

FACT:

It takes about 400 pounds of coal a year to keep one 100-watt light bulb burning 12 hours a day.

WHAT TO DO:

Check all the lamps in your house to see what size bulb is in each one. On top of the bulb is a number like 60W or 100W. This tells you how many "watts" (how much electric energy) a bulb uses. The higher the number, the more light the bulb gives, but the more energy it uses. Use a lower watt bulb if you don't need more light. If you need more light, remember that one 100-watt bulb gives more light, and uses less energy, than two 60-watt bulbs. And remind your parents that frosted bulbs give more light for the same amount of energy than soft-light bulbs.

AWARD BADGE:

I check all the bulbs in the house.

I Helped Save the Earth!

21. Use Less Paper

FACT:

American offices throw away enough paper every year to build a wall 12 feet high across the country. But, right now, we save 200 million trees a year by recycling.

WHAT TO DO:

Most paper thrown away in the office just has printing on one side. Ask your parents to bring home some of this paper so you can use the blank side for writing or drawing. Or cut it into smaller sizes and staple it together to make note pads.

AWARD BADGE:

I have my father or mother bring home office paper that would have been thrown away, and I find good uses for it.

I Helped Save the Earth!

22. Pick Up Litter

FACT:

Litter is not only ugly, but it can be harmful to wildlife. Small animals can get hurt on sharp cans or broken bottles, or get sick from eating plastic food packaging.

WHAT TO DO:

Pick up litter you see as you are walking. Throw away trash; recycle bottles and cans.

AWARD BADGE:

I pick up litter whenever I see it.

I Helped Save the Earth!

23. Recycle Bottles

FACT:

Americans throw out 25 billion bottles and jars every year. It takes a lot less energy to recycle a bottle than to make a new one.

WHAT TO DO:

Get two large boxes to hold bottles and jars for recycling. You will need to separate clear and colored glass. Put the boxes out of the way in a closet or the basement or garage. Wash out empty bottles and jars and put them in the correct box. Get someone to help you take them to the recycling center every few weeks.

AWARD BADGE:

I recycle bottles.

I Helped Save the Earth!

24. Get a Live Christmas Tree

FACT:

A cut Christmas tree is no longer taking carbon dioxide out of the air. And when it decays or is burned, it will release all the carbon dioxide it has removed in the past.

WHAT TO DO:

Get a tree in a pot. A small one won't cost any more than a cut tree at a Christmas tree lot. After Christmas, remove the decorations and plant it in your yard. You may have to wait until warmer weather if you live where it is very cold.

AWARD BADGE:

We get a live tree for Christmas.

I Helped Save the Earth!

25. Cut Down on Trips in the Car

FACT:

An automobile puts out its own weight in pollution every year. Most of that pollution is carbon dioxide, the biggest cause of global warming.

WHAT TO DO:

Don't ask your parents to drive you some place when you could walk or ride your bike. Plan your shopping so your parents can take you when they are going. Use the phone to help cut out unnecessary trips. Call ahead to make sure the store is open and that it has what you want.

AWARD BADGE:

I don't ask my parents to drive me anywhere
unless it is really necessary.

I Helped Save the Earth!

26. Turn Down the Heat and Adjust the Air Conditioner

FACT:

If every home in America turned down the heat by 4 degrees, we would save almost 400,000 barrels of oil a day. We could also save large amounts of energy by limiting the air conditioning in the summertime.

WHAT TO DO:

Ask your parents to turn down the thermostat during the heating season. Most people keep their homes warmer than they really need to. About 68 degrees is plenty warm if you dress right. In the summer, keep your air conditioner set at about 75 degrees.

AWARD BADGE:

We keep the heat turned down to a low temperature and the air conditioner turned up to a high temperature.

I Helped Save the Earth!

27. Don't Use the Hose to Wash Off the Sidewalk or Driveway

FACT:

When you turn on the hose, you use about 3 to 5 gallons of water a minute.

WHAT TO DO:

Don't use the garden hose to clean the sidewalk or the driveway. Use a broom instead.

AWARD BADGE:

I always use a broom to clean the sidewalk or driveway.

I Helped Save the Earth!

28. Don't Put Clean Clothes in the Laundry

FACT:

A washing machine uses over 5,000 gallons of water a year.

WHAT TO DO:

If the clothes you are wearing are clean, hang them up when you take them off. Don't throw them in the wash or drop them on the floor where they will get dirty and wrinkled and end up in the wash.

AWARD BADGE:

I take care of my clothes so they don't have to be washed as often.

I Helped Save the Earth!

29. Don't Buy Drinks in Plastic Containers

FACT:

Americans use 2.5 million plastic bottles every hour. These bottles can't be recycled and won't ever degrade.

WHAT TO DO:

Only buy soda and other drinks in aluminum cans or glass bottles. Buy milk or juice in cartons. Then recycle the container when you are done.

AWARD BADGE:

I try not to buy drinks in plastic containers.

I Helped Save the Earth!

30. Hang Up Your Wet Towels After Showers or Swimming

FACT:

The average family of four uses about 35 gallons of water a day just for washing clothes.

WHAT TO DO:

Hang your wet towels neatly on the towel rack so they can dry quickly. You'll be able to use them again, and cut down on the water and energy used for washing.

AWARD BADGE:

I always hang my wet towels on the towel rack.

I Helped Save the Earth!

31. Be Careful Using the Refrigerator

FACT:

It can cost 50 to 150 dollars a year for electricity to run the refrigerator.

WHAT TO DO:

Keep the door closed as much as possible. If you are making your lunch, think about everything you are going to need from the refrigerator, and get it all out at once. If you are putting things away after a meal, put all the stuff next to the refrigerator, then put it all in at once.

AWARD BADGE:

I am always careful to keep the refrigerator door open as little as I can.

I Helped Save the Earth!

32. Leave the Bag at the Store

FACT:

Half of the trash we throw out every day is packaging.

WHAT TO DO:

When you buy one or two small things, you don't need a bag to carry them. Tell that to the clerk. Just put it in your pocket or purse, or in a bag you already have for something else.

AWARD BADGE:

I never use a bag if I don't need one.

I Helped Save the Earth!

33. Buy Things Packaged in Cardboard, Not Plastic

FACT:

Most cardboard packaging is made out of recycled paper, and even if it isn't, it can be recycled.

WHAT TO DO:

If two different brands are about the same, but one is packed in cardboard and one is packed in plastic, buy the one packed in cardboard.

AWARD BADGE:

I always think about the packaging when I buy something.

I Helped Save the Earth!

34. Put All the Trash in One Bag

FACT:

Plastic trash bags cost money, never degrade, and can't be recycled.

WHAT TO DO:

Is it your job to go through the house on trash day and empty all the wastebaskets? Don't just grab the plastic bag full of trash out of each basket. If the bag is clean, dump the trash into one big bag you carry with you, and leave the clean bag in the wastebasket to be used again. Best of all, use a paper bag to collect all that trash, not plastic.

AWARD BADGE:

I don't waste trash bags.

I Helped Save the Earth!

35. Don't Let the Water Run While Washing the Car

FACT:

Leaving the hose on while washing the car can waste 100 to 150 gallons of water.

WHAT TO DO:

Fill a bucket with soapy water and wash the car with a sponge. Turn on the hose to rinse off the car, and turn it off again right away.

AWARD BADGE:

I don't waste water when I wash the car.

I Helped Save the Earth!

36. Make Sure All Outdoor Lights Are Out During the Day

FACT:

Lighting an average light bulb for a year creates about 1000 pounds of carbon dioxide and other gases.

WHAT TO DO:

Check the lights on your porch, patio or deck before you go to bed to make sure that they are turned off if no one is using them. Double check them in the morning to make sure that they are not on all day.

AWARD BADGE:

I check the outdoor lights to make sure they are off.

I Helped Save the Earth!

37. Don't Buy Disposable Products

FACT:

Americans throw out about 1000 pounds of garbage per person every year.

WHAT TO DO:

Cut down on your garbage by not buying things that are made to be used once and thrown away. This includes everything from paper plates to disposable cameras.

AWARD BADGE:

I try not to buy disposable products,
but if I must I will make sure they are degradable.

I Helped Save the Earth!

38. Keep Glass Fireplace Doors Closed

FACT:

Hot air rises. The heat in your home rises right up the chimney.

WHAT TO DO:

Keep the glass doors on your fireplace closed at all times. This is even more important when you do have a fire burning. The heat from the fire going up the chimney takes the heat from the house with it, even faster than with no fire. Glass doors keep the heat in the house.

AWARD BADGE:

I always make sure the fireplace doors are closed.

I Helped Save the Earth!

39. Carpool With Your Friends When You Are Going Out

FACT:

Cars produce carbon monoxide, which causes air pollution, smog, and serious health problems.

WHAT TO DO:

Don't arrange to meet your friends at the mall or the movie or wherever you are going. Have your parents take you and your friends wherever you are going, and have someone else's parents pick you all up.

AWARD BADGE:

My friends and I carpool to movies and other places we go.

I Helped Save the Earth!

40. Start a Compost Heap in Your Backyard

FACT:

If every American family that gardens started a compost heap, we would eliminate 20 percent of our solid waste.

WHAT TO DO:

Start a compost heap in your backyard, using kitchen scraps, leaves, grass clippings, and other organic material. Composting is a process that turns these waste materials into valuable fertilizer. Check the library or bookstore for instructions.

AWARD BADGE:

I maintain a compost heap in my backyard.

I Helped Save the Earth!

41. Turn Down the Water Heater

FACT:

Most home water heaters are set higher than they should be, wasting energy and costing money.

WHAT TO DO:

Make sure the water heater in your house is set to the lowest setting. And turn off the water heater when you go on a long trip.

AWARD BADGE:

Our water heater is turned down low,
and we turn it off when we go on vacation.

I Helped Save the Earth!

42. Check the Water Meter For Leaks

FACT:

About one-fifth of our water is lost before we use it. It leaks out through broken pipes or loose joints.

WHAT TO DO:

Find out where the water meter is. This measures the water level. Write down the meter reading on a day when no one will be home to use water. Check the reading again when you get home, before anyone uses the water. If the number has changed, there is a water leak somewhere. Tell an adult, so they can have the utility company fix this.

AWARD BADGE:

I check the water meter for leaks in my house.

I Helped Save the Earth!

43. Put Garbage in Compost or Trash, Not in Disposal

FACT:

Putting food scraps in the garbage disposal uses a lot of water, and it puts garbage into the water that has to be removed by the sewage plant.

WHAT TO DO:

Put the scraps in the trash. Even better, put them in a compost heap.

AWARD BADGE:

I don't put scraps or garbage in the disposal.

I Helped Save the Earth!

44. Don't Buy Products in Small, Non-refillable Containers

FACT:

About one dollar out of every ten we spend goes to pay for packaging.

WHAT TO DO:

Don't buy products that come in small, non-refillable containers. Buy things like shampoo that come in refillable containers, or save the small bottles. Then buy the largest sizes available, and refill the small containers. You save money by buying larger sizes. And the larger size uses one large plastic bottle instead of three or four small ones.

AWARD BADGE:

I buy things that come in refillable containers whenever I can.

I Helped Save the Earth!

45. Repair or Recycle Your Old Stuff; Fix it, Donate it, or Have a Garage Sale Rather Than Throwing Things Away

FACT:

Your old toy can be a new toy for someone else. And it doesn't use up energy to make it or packaging to sell it.

WHAT TO DO:

When your parents make you get rid of those old toys you haven't played with in years, don't throw them in the garbage. Have a garage sale or trade them with friends for something you want. Or take them to Goodwill or the Salvation Army so other kids can get some fun out of them.

AWARD BADGE:

I recycle my old toys.

I Helped Save the Earth!

46. Take Your Vending Machine Cans or Bottles Home For Recycling

FACT:

Recycling at home is only half the job. You probably use as many cans or bottles away from home as you do at home.

WHAT TO DO:

When you buy a can of soda for lunch or a snack at school, wash out the can (so it doesn't get sticky) and put it in your backpack or gym bag or lunchbox. Take it home and add it to the cans you are recycling there. Or start a recycling program at school. Ask your teachers to help. Get a couple of large trash cans and put up signs that they are for recyclable cans only.

AWARD BADGE:

I recycle aluminum cans at school.

I Helped Save the Earth!

47. Leave the Grass Clippings on the Lawn

FACT:

Grass clippings just use up plastic bags and fill up landfills that much faster. And they are good for the lawn.

WHAT TO DO:

Ask your parents if you can leave the bag off the lawn mower. The mower will spread the clippings evenly over the lawn and they will not be noticeable. You will have to sweep off the driveway and the sidewalks when you are through. The other good thing to do with clippings is to put them in a compost heap.

AWARD BADGE:

I leave the clippings on the lawn, or put them in a compost heap.

I Helped Save the Earth!

48. Check the Temperature in Your Refrigerator

FACT:

Most people keep their refrigerators and freezers much colder than they have to.

WHAT TO DO:

Get an outdoor thermometer and put it in the refrigerator for about 10 minutes. Then check it. It should be about 40 degrees. This is cold enough to keep the food from spoiling. Then check the temperature in the freezer. It should be about 5 degrees above zero. If your refrigerator or freezer is set too low, ask an adult to show you how to turn them up.

AWARD BADGE:

I check the temperature in the refrigerator and freezer every two months.

I Helped Save the Earth!

49. Pull the Weeds, Don't Spray Them

FACT:

Weed sprays are toxic. Eventually some of the poison gets back into the water system, where it harms plants and animals. If there is enough used, even humans can suffer.

WHAT TO DO:

Don't use weed spray. Pull the weeds out by the roots, or use a special weeding tool to dig them up.

AWARD BADGE:

I don't use weed spray when I help in the garden.

I Helped Save the Earth!

50. Don't Use Aerosol Products

FACT:

Aerosols are made with harmful gases that destroy the ozone layer which screens out harmful rays of the sun.

WHAT TO DO:

Don't buy hairspray or other products that come in aerosol cans. Buy the brands that come in spray bottles with pumps or other applicators.

AWARD BADGE:

I don't buy aerosol products.

I Helped Save the Earth!

51. Pack Your School Lunch in Reusable Containers

FACT:

Less than one percent of plastic is recycled today.

WHAT TO DO:

Take your lunch to school in a lunchbox. (It doesn't have to look like a lunchbox or have pictures of Mickey Mouse on it.) Or carry it in a backpack or gym bag. Or carry it in a plastic bag and bring the bag home to use again and again. Put your sandwiches in an airtight plastic sandwich container instead of throwaway plastic bags. The sandwich box is made of plastic, but it can be used hundreds and hundreds of times.

AWARD BADGE:

I pack my lunch in reusable containers.

I Helped Save the Earth!

52. Clean Your Dryer Lint Screen Regularly

FACT:

A clogged lint screen makes the dryer work much harder, using up to twenty percent more energy to dry a load of clothes.

WHAT TO DO:

Help out on wash day. Find out where the lint screen is on your dryer and how to clean it. Check it after every load or two and make sure to remove all the lint.

AWARD BADGE:

I keep the lint screen clean on our dryer.

I Helped Save the Earth!

53. Don't Throw Your Old Batteries in the Trash

FACT:

Americans throw out 2.5 billion pounds of batteries a year. Toxic chemicals in batteries can be released into the environment, especially if they are burned.

WHAT TO DO:

Save your old batteries and take them to a recycling center or give them to your community's toxic waste clean-up program.

AWARD BADGE:

I don't throw old batteries in the trash.

I Helped Save the Earth!

54. Talk to Your Parents About What They Can Do to Help Save the Earth

FACT:

You can do a lot to help save the earth, but your parents have to take care of the big things like the car and the furnace and so on.

WHAT TO DO:

Talk to your parents about helping to save the earth. Tell them about what you are doing, and why it is important. Help them think up ways to help save the earth.

AWARD BADGE:

I talked to my parents about how they can help save the earth.

I Helped Save the Earth!

55. Come Up With Your Own Way to Help Save the Earth

FACT:

You can help other kids help save the earth.

WHAT TO DO:

Come up with your own way to help save the earth. Write it down and mail it to:

Michael O'Brian
I HELPED SAVE THE EARTH
c/o Boldface Publishing
P.O. Box 3685
Omaha, Nebraska 68103

Include your name and address. If yours is one of the better ones, it may be printed in our next book, and you will be listed as the one who came up with the idea.

AWARD BADGE:

I thought of my own way to help save the earth.

I Helped Save the Earth!